Color this page to make it your own. Then find things to color throughout the book!

Jesus came to teach all people about the kingdom of God—*especially* those who were sinners. But not everyone was happy about this—*especially* the Pharisees and scribes.

One day, the Pharisees and the scribes were grumbling about Jesus. "He talks to sinners!" they exclaimed. "And He even eats with them!"

So Jesus told them this parable (a story with a special meaning):

"If a man has one hundred sheep and loses one, what does he do? He leaves the ninety-nine to search for the lost one. When he finds it, he puts it on his shoulders and happily carries it home. Then he calls out to all his friends and neighbors, 'Come and celebrate with me! I've found my lost sheep!'

"It's the same way in heaven," said Jesus. "There is more joy over one sinner who turns back to God than over the ninety-nine who didn't turn away from Him."

Then Jesus asked, "If a woman has ten silver coins and loses one of them, what does she do? She lights a lamp, sweeps out the whole house, and searches everywhere until she finds it. And when she does find it, she calls all her friends and neighbors together and says, 'Be happy for me! I've found my lost coin!'

"In the same way," Jesus said to the Pharisees and scribes, "the angels in heaven celebrate over one sinner who turns back to God."

Jesus then told them this parable about a father and his two sons:

"A man had two sons. One day, the younger son said to his father, 'Father, give me my share of your fortune now.' This made the father very sad, but he gave the son his share of the family's fortune.

"Just a few days later, the younger son gathered up all his belongings and left. He traveled to a far-away country, where he wasted all his money on foolish living.

"After the younger son had spent all his money, a terrible famine stuck that land. He had no money and no food and no friends. He had to go to work in the fields, feeding pigs. He was *so* hungry that he longed to eat the pigs' food, but no one would even give him any of that!

"One day, the son said to himself, 'I am dying of hunger, but even my father's servants have more than enough food to eat! I'll go back to my father and say to him, "Father, I have sinned against you and against heaven. I'm not worthy to be called your son. Just let me be like one of your servants."'

"Then the son got up and began the long journey back home to his father.

"While the son was still a long way off, his father saw him coming, and his heart was filled with love and compassion. The father ran to him, threw his arms around his neck, and kissed him.

"'Father,' the son said, 'I have sinned against you and against heaven. I'm not even worthy to be called your son.'

"But his father called to his servants and said, 'Quick! Bring out the best robe, and put it on my son. Bring a ring for his finger and sandals for his feet. Then kill the fattened calf, and let's have a great feast to celebrate! My son was lost to me, but now he is found again!' And so they began to celebrate.

"Now the older son had been out in the fields. When he came home, he heard all the music and dancing. 'What's going on?' he asked one of the servants.

"'Your younger brother has come home!' the servant told him. 'And your father is having a great feast to celebrate because he has his son back, safe and sound.'

"But the older brother wasn't happy—he was angry! And he refused to go in to the feast. His father came out and pleaded with him to come in. But the brother said, 'I have worked for you for years. I've done everything you've ever asked, but you never gave me even a young goat to have a small feast with my friends. But when this son who took your money and left comes home, you have a great feast for him!'

"'My son,' the father said, 'everything I have is yours. But I had to celebrate. Your brother was lost to me, but now he is found!'"

Jesus didn't come to save only the good people or the people who already know about God. He came to save all who turn from sin and trust in Him. Even when we were still sinners, He died for you and me. Now He calls us to trust Him as Savior and obey Him as Lord.

"The Son of Man has come to seek and to save the lost."
—*Luke 19:10*

Jesus was no ordinary man. He was—and is—the Son of God! He was with God before the earth was created, and as the Son of God, Jesus has power over all creation. And the good news is that the One who controls creation is the same One who loves you and me!

[Jesus] was with God in the beginning.
All things were created through Him, and apart from Him
not one thing was created that has been created.
—John 1:2–3

Jesus and Peter stepped into the boat. As soon as they did, the wind stopped its howling and the sea became calm. The disciples all worshipped Jesus and said, "Truly You are the Son of God!"

Could it really be Jesus? the disciples wondered.

"Lord, if it's really You," Peter called out, "tell me to come to You on the water."

"Come!" Jesus said.

So Peter carefully climbed out of the boat. He set first one foot and then the other on top of the water. Then Peter was walking on the water too! But when he looked around him, he saw the wind and waves. He was afraid, and he began to sink. Terrified, Peter cried out, "Lord, save me!"

Immediately Jesus reached out His hand and pulled Peter up. "Why did you doubt?" Jesus asked him.

Around three in the morning, Jesus came walking out toward His disciples in the boat. He was walking on water! When the disciples saw Him, they were terrified. "It's a ghost!" they cried out in fear.

But Jesus called out to them, "Have courage! It is I. Don't be afraid."

After the people left, Jesus went up on the mountain by Himself to pray. When evening came, He was there alone. The disciples' boat was already out in the middle of the sea. The wind had begun to blow, and the sea was churning. The wind and the waves battered against the disciples' boat.

After this, Jesus told the disciples to get back in the boat. He wanted them to sail on ahead of Him to the other side while He said good-bye to the crowds of people.

The people sat down and waited to see what would happen. Jesus took the five loaves and the two fish. Then, looking up to heaven, He gave thanks for them. He broke the loaves and gave them to the disciples, and the disciples gave them to the crowds. Jesus also divided the fish among all the people.

Everyone ate as much as they wanted. And the disciples still picked up twelve baskets full of leftover pieces—all from five small loaves and two little fish!

So Jesus said, "How many loaves do you have? Go and see."

After searching, one of His disciples, named Andrew (who was Peter's brother), said, "There's a boy here who has five small loaves and two fish. But how can we feed so many people with so little food?"

Jesus simply said, "Bring them here to Me."

Now there was plenty of grass in that place, so Jesus said to the disciples, "Have the people sit down in groups of about fifty."

But Philip, one of the twelve disciples, said, "It would take more than a year's pay to buy even a little bit of bread for this many people!" (For there were about 5,000 men gathered there, plus all the women and children.)

Now the place where Jesus was teaching was out in the country, away from the towns. So when evening came, the disciples went to Jesus and said, "This place is a wilderness, and it's already late. Send the people away so they can go into the villages and buy food for themselves."

"They don't need to go away," Jesus said. "You give them something to eat."

They ran along the shore so that they reached the other side—even before Jesus and His disciples!

Jesus stepped out of the boat and saw all the people. His heart hurt for them because they were like sheep without a shepherd. So He began to heal their sick and to teach them.

Jesus sent His disciples out to teach the people about the coming of God's kingdom. When they returned, they wanted to tell Him all about everything they had seen and heard and done. But people were coming and going all around them. The disciples didn't even have time to eat! Jesus saw how very tired and hungry they were, so He said, "Let's go away by ourselves so you can rest."

They were near the Sea of Galilee, so they all got into a boat and sailed toward the other side. But the crowds of people saw where they were going.

Color this page to make it your own. Then find things to color throughout the book!